16.95

16.95

The Hidden Life of the
MEADOW

Photographs by DWIGHT KUHN
Text by DAVID M. SCHWARTZ

CROWN PUBLISHERS, INC.
NEW YORK

To my son David and his friend Chris Jones
for their special love of nature.
D.K.

For the memory of my grandmothers, Sarah and Pearl.
D.M.S.

Text copyright © 1988 by David Schwartz
Photographs copyright © 1988 by Dwight Kuhn

Concept development and photo/editorial coordination
by the Soderstrom Publishing Group Inc.

Published by Crown Publishers, Inc., 225 Park Avenue South, New York, New
York 10003 and represented in Canada by the Canadian MANDA Group
Limited

CROWN is a trademark of Crown Publishers, Inc.

Manufactured in Japan

Book design by Kathleen Westray and Ed Sturmer

Library of Congress Cataloging-in-Publication Data

Kuhn, Dwight. The hidden life of the meadow/photographs by Dwight Kuhn;
text by David M. Schwartz.

Summary: Photographs and text introduce the animals, plants, and ecology of a
meadow.

1. Meadow fauna—Juvenile literature. 2. Meadow plants—Juvenile literature.
3. Meadow ecology—Juvenile literature. [1. Meadow animals. 2. Meadow plants.
3. Meadow ecology. 4. Ecology.] I. Schwartz, David M. II. Title.
QL115.5.K84 1988   574.5′2643—dc19   88-14934

ISBN 0-517-57059-9

10 9 8 7 6 5 4 3 2 1

First Edition

White-footed mouse

In winter, the meadow appears silent, bleak, and still.
If you bundled up and walked through it, you might
think you were alone. But underneath the snow there is
a maze of tunnels—a highway system for small animals
in search of roots and seeds. During a brief thaw, this
white-footed mouse peers above the snow. It has made
itself a warm nest in an old tree stump.

Pussywillows give one of the first clues of warmer days ahead. Snow may still spot the ground when the pussywillow opens its buds to reveal furry clusters called catkins. A little later, when warm days finally arrive, flowers will push through the catkins' gray silk.

Pussywillow with catkins

Pussywillow with flowers

Soon, the first blooms of spring blanket the meadow: dandelions, dandelions, dandelions everywhere. Where did they all come from? It may be hard to believe, but seeds from one dandelion plant can create a meadow like this in just a few years.

Dandelion

White-footed mouse with newborn young

With warm weather, the white-footed mouse bears blind and helpless young in its grass-lined nest. The newborns become fat and furry in less than two weeks.

In just two months, the young mice will be nearly full grown. By then their gray coats will have turned brown. A white-footed mouse may have four litters a year, each with one to seven offspring.

Unlike mice, snowshoe hares are born open-eyed and ready to run off. This one has hopped up to a ready-made meal. Its dark color helps it hide in the grass and leaves, but next winter it will turn white to blend with the snow. As winter approaches, snowshoe hares grow a thick mat of hair between their toes to help support them on the soft snow.

Several-week-old snowshoe hare

Meadow vole

A one-acre meadow may have anywhere from three hundred to twelve thousand meadow voles, but they are difficult to spot. You are more likely to see the winding tunnels they chew through the grass. Voles are stockier than mice, with shorter tails and smaller ears. They are active year-round, day and night.

Hummingbird

Another active meadow creature is the hummingbird. With its long and slender beak and even longer tongue, a hummingbird can reach deep into a flower's petals to sip its nectar. Where does it perch, then? Nowhere! Unlike other birds, "hummers" can hover in place, helicopter-style. The bird's humming sound comes from its wings beating from fifty to seventy times a second!

If you ever see a foamy mass of bubbles on a stem, take a closer look—you'll probably see a spittlebug inside. Young spittlebugs have soft skin, and to keep from drying out, they surround themselves with foam. By the time the spittlebug grows into an adult, it develops hard skin and wings and will fly away.

Spittlebug

Killdeer

On a low rocky spot at the edge of a meadow, a killdeer sits on her eggs, keeping them warm for more than three weeks. When her babies hatch, they will look like miniature versions of herself, immediately able to hop around and peck at food—and get into trouble if a raccoon or other predator should happen along.

Two-day-old killdeer

The killdeer has a clever way of protecting her young. First she distracts the predator with an ear-splitting call, *Kill-deer, kill-deer.* Then she pretends to have a broken wing so the predator will think she's an easy meal. Dragging her wing along the ground, the mother leads the predator farther and farther astray, until her young are safe. Then she gives up her act and flies off, leaving the predator behind—and still hungry.

Killdeer mother in broken wing act

Walk quietly along the edge of the meadow
and you may hear an unmistakable song:
Witchity-witchity-witchity-witch! It is the
song of the yellow throat, a type of warbler
that nests low in the grasses of meadows
and marshes. Male yellow throats have a
distinctive black mask around their eyes.

Yellow-throat warbler

Savannah sparrow

This male savannah sparrow uses its voice in many ways. With one song it claims a territory and warns other males, "If you come here I will drive you away!" With another song the male attracts a female. While the female nests, he sings to tell her where he is and to mark their territorial boundary so other sparrows won't come too close.

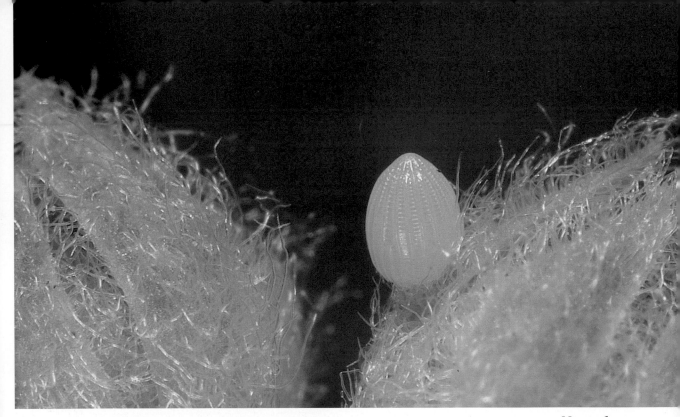

Monarch egg

Monarch caterpillar

On a sunny day in early summer, a monarch mother alights on a milkweed plant to cement her pinhead-sized egg to a milkweed plant.

After chewing its way out of the egg, the monarch caterpillar becomes an "eating machine," devouring every milkweed leaf it can get its jaws on. The bitter milkweed sap makes the caterpillar taste terrible to predators. Once a robin or bluejay has eaten a monarch caterpillar, it will never try one again.

After two weeks of feeding, the caterpillar forms a hard shell around itself. At this stage in its life it is called a chrysalis. Although you cannot see through the surface at first, gradually it turns clear. Eventually, the shell splits open and out comes a fully formed adult.

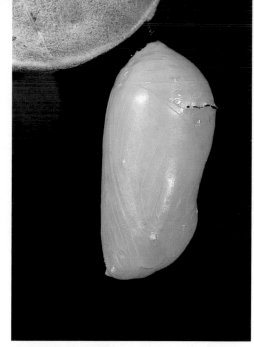

Monarch chrysalis

Developing chrysalis

Monarch butterfly

Dandelion

By late spring, the bright yellow dandelions have turned into big, round blowballs of grayish fluff. Actually, they're not all fluff. At the base of each silky parachute is a tiny brown fruit containing a single seed. The whole parachute is ready to ride away with the slightest breeze.

With spring rains and increased daylight, many plants have a growth spurt. Uncut, weeds can reach a height of three or four feet by midsummer.

Sun and weeds

Aphids on a plant

Hunched over like football players, tiny insects called aphids use their sharp beaks like straws to drink the juices of many plants. Aphids are so small that eight of them in a line would stretch only one inch.

If every aphid were to survive, an aphid mother would have six hundred billion great-great-great-great-great-great-great grandchildren in just one summer! Together they would weigh as much as ten thousand humans.

Fortunately, the aphids have many predators. One is the ladybug. Ladybugs are so good at eating tiny plant-sucking insects that just ten of them and their offspring can clean several million aphids off a badly infested tree in just a few months.

Ladybug

The grasshopper is another common insect pest, too large to fall prey to a ladybug, but an easy catch for the powerful praying mantis.

Grasshopper

Praying mantis

Like ladybugs, praying mantises are helpful to people because they eat destructive insects. In some places it is against the law to kill a mantis.

Wild lupines

White admiral butterfly

Tall, showy spikes of lupines add more than color to a meadow. Their roots add a natural fertilizer to the soil.

The same insect can be both friend and enemy to plants. Caterpillars chew up plants, but adult butterflies carry pollen from one flower to another. Without them many plants could not set seeds.

A common sight in open grassland, woodchucks are slow runners, but they are not an easy catch. At the first sign of danger they emit a high, piercing whistle to warn other woodchucks, and then scoot into an underground burrow.

Woodchuck

By summer, every meadow has its share of horseflies— perhaps more than you would wish. You may see only one fly at a time, but a fly sees thousands of you! That's because the fly's eyes have thousands of lenses so it can see in thousands of different directions at once. The rain-bowlike stripes of color are created by the many lenses acting as a prism.

Horsefly

Garden spider

Even though spiders have eight eyes, each eye is tiny and it has only one lens. But poor vision doesn't keep spiders from catching prey. Many weave webs of silk. To lure flying insects, a garden spider weaves a shiny zigzag band through the middle of its web, then it moves to the side to wait.

Crab spider capturing honeybee

A single meadow may contain two million spiders. The crab spider spins no web, but it has other ways of capturing prey—in this case, a honeybee. Deep inside a blossom, a crab spider waits for an insect to come sip a flower's nectar. When it lands, the spider pounces upon it.

Young fox

Foxes are shy and secretive, waiting until the coast is clear before treading out of the woods in search of mice, voles, and other small prey. Even though they are a help to mankind because they prey upon so many pests, foxes have been completely killed off in many areas.

Browsing in meadow clover, this fawn may give you a clue as to why young deer have spots. The spots will disappear by fall. Despite their beauty, deer like to feed on orchards, gardens, and farms, so some people consider them pests.

Fawn

Chipmunk

This chipmunk had best watch out or it might fall prey to a wily fox. If it's quick enough, it can outfox the fox by ducking into an underground burrow. Great horders of food, chipmunks carry fruit and seeds in their cheek pouches and deposit them in special hideaways.

Green snake

Garter snake

Snakes flick their tongues to sniff the air. The forked tongue doesn't actually do the smelling. The tongue transports scent from the air to two tiny pockets at the top of the snake's mouth. These pockets act as the snake's "nose." Snakes are not slimy, as many people think. In fact, a snake's scales must be hard and dry, or the snake would not be able to move quickly over grass, logs, and rocks. The green snake and garter snake are common in meadows and gardens. They are not to be feared—unless you are a frog or a mouse. Then you might be a meal!

Just as dandelions dotted the springtime meadow, the late summer meadow is painted yellow with goldenrod.

Like the vole, the short-tail shrew is abundant but rarely seen. Here, it has lifted its head after sipping water from a cupped leaf. Shrews are among the smallest mammals on earth. One species weighs less than a dime! The short-tail is a "heavyweight" by comparison—it weighs about the same as three quarters.

Shrew

Bumblebee

Bumblebees are among our most valuable insects. They pollinate watermelon, cantaloupe, cranberries, and squash, in addition to many wildflowers.

Worker bees drink flower nectar, then spit it into a waxy "honeypot." Honeypots are like storage tanks for the liquid food that the entire colony depends on during bad weather. The largest bee is the queen.

Bumblebee sipping nectar

Bumblebee colony

Colder weather and shorter days splash the trees with brilliant colors, but many meadow plants simply turn brown and wither on the stalk. Most of those that stay green through autumn will die with the first hard frost. But they leave seeds and roots behind to assure that more plants will reappear next spring.

White-footed mouse

An early snowfall both helps and hinders the meadow's inhabitants in their search for food. Branches may sag or break under the weight of snow, putting berries and other foods within easy reach.